The Art of the Political Campaign

Brian Duewel

How to run for elected office with no money, name recognition or political connections

The Ultimate Guide on Political Campaigning.

Naperville, Illinois

What others are saying about this book:

"...of course the experiences bring back many memories - I know what it's like to manage an operation on a shoestring - a great read for those thinking about public life. In the words from Chapter Four, 'Just do it.' Next, I'd like to catch up to some to the folks Brian writes about: what are their plans for the year 2013?"

Thom Serafin.

Political Consultant,
Former Staffer for U.S. Senator Alan Dixon,
& Former Press Secretary for a U.S. Presidential Campaign

"Even for those of us who follow politics closely, this book is an absolute eye-opener. This is more than just political campaigning up-close and personal; it's from the inside out."

Roger Brown.

Broadcast Journalist,
Chicago, Illinois

"For anyone thinking about running for elected office, this book is a no brainer. Not only will it save you dozens of hours in trial and error, but you'll probably save thousands of dollars by avoiding all the costly mistakes Brian points out."

Dan Barile.

Political Activist
Chicago, Illinois

The Art of the Political Campaign

How to run for elected office with no money, name recognition or political connections.

First Edition

Brian Duewel
Naperville, Illinois

Title: The Art of the Political Campaign

Subtitle: How to run for elected office with no money, name recognition or political connections
Author: Brian Duewel
Publisher: Brian Duewel

Copyright © 2013 by Brian Duewel
First Edition, 2013
Published in the United States of America

Table of Contents

Sharon Goldsworthy

Tom Hansen

Donnalee Lozeau

Rick Taylor

Gary Fuller

W. Suzanne Handshoe

Bill Swintkowski

Doug Pierce

Scott Mangold

Bucky Johnson

Wayne Silas

Tony Petelos

Suzanne Atwell

Donnie Henriques

Brian Landers

George Scherck

Leonard Urban

Brian Grim

Tommy Allegood

Earl Jaques, Jr.

Ruth Briggs King

Mathias Harter

Jim DeCesare

Brent Yonts

Robert Byrnes

Mike Winder

Paul C. Lambi

Jim Farley

Scott Eckstein

Dick Gleason

Bill Otto

Bob Hartwell

Mike Gabbard

Tamara Jenkins

Jerry Miller

Frank Lucente

Harry Parrish

Peter Corroon

Charles Langlinais

Joe Markley

Carolyn Eslick

Dave Kiffer

Barbara Bollier

Shari Buck

Part 3: Securing a political appointment

Philip Murphy

Jim Reynolds

Preface

I first made my move into the political arena back in the summer of 2009. It was a goal I had always set for myself. As a child, I wanted to be mayor of the small town where I grew up. I'm not sure if it was a call to civic duty or the desire to make something out of my life. Either way, it was something I knew I had to do.

I had worked in television production from the time I graduated college through that summer in 2009. That was when, like millions of other Americans, I was laid-off. At the time, I was also a small business owner, freelance writer and teacher. Because of my experience, I thought I had all the traits needed to represent my neighbors on my county board.

Although I continued working as a freelance producer in the television industry, the lay-off freed me to make my run for office. Since I previously worked full-time for a news outlet, I was barred from political life. The appearance of a conflict of interest held me back; politics and news reporting just don't mix. Thanks to the recession, I was now self-employed... that made me free to attempt my goal.

In July 2009, I announced my intention to win a seat on the DuPage (Illinois) County Board.

What a Learning Process

During the campaign, I was shocked by how much I didn't know about campaigning. In fact, I didn't even know how to find the answers.

From approaching my local party, to filing papers and fundraising, it was all so foreign. I felt there had to be a place to look for answers, but everywhere I turned, I found more questions.

The Book Decision

With years of writing experience behind me, I decided early on in the process, that I was going to document my experiences and share them with future want-to-be politicians. When the 15 month experiment was over, I had one major problem with my campaign memoirs.

I received nearly 40% of the vote. My opponent received 60%.

Who would completely trust campaign tips from someone who lost his only race? For a short period of time, this kept me from advancing my product. But the more I thought about it, the more I realized the need for this service. I pondered extensively and searched for a solution.

I believe I found it.

This book is a compilation of experiences - the first four chapters are my personal thoughts and guidance – the rest of the book is advice from already elected officials.

I made it a point to include politicians from all across the country, from mayors and state senators to county board members and state representatives. I purposely focused on the smaller offices, because it's my experience that people running for these smaller positions have less knowledge and need more help. Once people get to "governor" and "U.S. Senator" status, they already know what they need, have a thick bankroll and have the team around them to achieve their goals.

This guide is meant to help the beginning to mid-level politician achieve his or her goals. Written in simple form for easy reference, this can be an invaluable resource for the budding elected official. From why to run for office and how to file the forms to how to prepare for debates and making the final push, it's all here in this tidy manual.

Obviously, I ran for office as a member of a political party, but I decided as I was writing, that I would keep that information out of the book. I've had people tell me that it's impossible to write a political book without mentioning parties, but I wanted to prove them wrong. And it's not just my party that I left out; I decided to avoid party mentions with any of the officials that volunteered a submission.

That's because, for me personally, one of the most important things about this book was to keep it politically free. I thought this was the best way to present all the submitted information. If someone reading this was a staunch conservative and they were to read a story about how a left-leaning mayor won his seat, they might not learn the real message. And vice-versa.

Therefore, quite simply, this is a book about campaigning, not about politics.

Part 1
My experiences, views and thoughts

Chapter 1

The First Step

Why run for office?

The first thing you want to ask yourself is, "Why do I want to run for public office." For me, it was a childhood dream. What is it for you? Is it to help your fellow man? A policy you want to change? Maybe a career objective you want to accomplish?

There are many reasons to run for office, but it's essential to know exactly why you're attempting the run. When you know why you're going through the process, you always have that reminder when times get tough.

The phrase, "It's not a sprint, it's a marathon," certainly applies to a political campaign. Even for small races, the process will last well over a year. That's months and months of meetings, events, fundraising, lunches and door-to-door canvassing. If you have another job or a family, this can be overwhelming. If you have the "Why am I doing this," answer to fall back on, you'll have the strength to push through the hard times.

Where there were stretches when I wanted to quit? Absolutely. I wanted to throw in the towel on numerous occasions. But every time I felt this way, I thought back to why I was doing it, and got a renewed sense of purpose.

What office? What party?

Early on, you need to decide what office you're running for and whether you have a political affiliation.

It goes without saying, but these are probably the two biggest decisions you're going to make running for office. It's hard to campaign without knowing what office for which you're running. Take plenty of time, figure out why you're doing what you're doing, and make the choices carefully. These are obvious questions you need to ask yourself, but they're important decisions that will influence your entire crusade.

The party decision is probably one that you will already have the answer to before you even think about running for office. Most people naturally lean either left (liberal) or right (conservative). If you truly don't know with which party you side, take some time to compare your feelings about issues with how each party feels about those same issues.

The local view of politics may be different than all of the national opinions, so think about the office you're seeking and how the local party folks see the issues important to the community. Talk to people; pick their brain and side with the party that most closely aligns with your feelings.

You may ask, "What if I'm an independent?" or "What if it's a non-partisan office?" I think that's great, because that's actually how I felt before my race. But here's the sad truth behind politics: without the support of one party or another, it's terribly difficult to win a race.

Think about how many politicians run for office each year... how many do you know that won their race as an independent? My guess is, "Not many." Usually the only ones who can successfully run as an independent are the people that have already made a name for themselves as either a Democrat or a Republican.

At this level, you'll need the support, advice and help of the smart and powerful people in your local party organization. So whether you like it or not, you should pick a side.

Understanding the timeline

It's important to understand the timeline that's involved in the political process. If you're reading this and its September or October, you shouldn't anticipate running for office until at least the following November. Even then, that's not enough time.

Ideally, for small town, county and district offices, you should plan out about 15-18 months. About 18 months prior to the election, you should begin the soul searching; that is, understanding why you're running.

It's in these early stages you'll begin thinking about all the other things that will need to be done, like hiring staff (or recruiting volunteers), securing office space and supplies, evaluate your opponent and his/her position and of course, getting on the ballot.

Getting on the ballot

Going into my campaign, I had no political experience, no political connections and no political allegiance. I was starting from point zero. After I was laid-off in 2009, I sat down with my wife, told her my intentions, and sat there clueless.

I knew what I was going to do and I knew why I was doing it, I just didn't know how. I asked my non-political wife if she knew what I should do next, she didn't. I asked my non-political friends if they knew the process; they didn't. I asked my non-political parents if they knew my next step; they didn't.

I didn't have too many friends or relatives that were into politics, so everywhere I looked, there were no answers.

For example, I didn't even know how to officially "announce" my candidacy. Should I call the local newspapers? Should I hold a press conference? I had no idea.

In fact, I didn't even know what official papers needed to be filed with the county to get on the ballot. Nobody in my circle of influence knew the answers either. All I really knew was that I wanted to hold a seat on the DuPage County Board.

After an internet search, I found that the next step is to approach your chosen political party. My search led me to my county party organization and my township organization. Since I was running for county board, I reached out to the president of the countywide party.

We met for lunch and discussed my options. This was the best decision I made the whole race. His advice and guidance meant I didn't have to go at it alone. Finally, I had people on my side. I had a "team."

I encourage you to do the same. Reach out to your local party for help and advice. In many cases, you'll also need their support and endorsement.

This becomes easier if there's not a candidate running for the office you're seeking in your party. If the party already has a "favorite son," your road is a lot tougher. If the party's decision is you or an empty ballot spot, they'll almost always choose you.

Luckily, I was the only candidate, so it was a fairly easy choice for the organization to support me.

Early on, the party held an information and paperwork night for all of the local candidates. We got together with a lawyer and filled out the proper forms to get us on the ballot. I also needed to understand the concept of petition signatures. With their help, I learned the number I would need to be official. The local office even delivered the papers and signatures to the county clerk.

If you don't have the backing of your party, or don't have a party altogether, you'll need to do all this alone. Contact your county clerk or check out the clerk's website for the proper forms to get you on the ballot. The rules differ from between jurisdictions, so you'll need guidance from local officials.

This can be intimidating and confusing, so I urge you to talk to your election officials so you don't make mistakes. A screw-up at this point might be the difference between being an official candidate and not making the ballot.

Once you have all your paperwork and signatures filled out and turned in, you're nearly official.

There's a grace period where anyone can look over your signatures and challenge your ballot entry. Again, this is where having your local party on your side is helpful. A couple of our countywide candidates had challenges to their signatures. The party lawyer oversaw the challenge and got the dispute thrown out. If you're alone, you'll have to defend yourself or hire your own lawyer.

Once you pass the challenge stage, you're an official candidate.

Follow your heart and mind during this stage and see it through. It's not always easy, but I believe it's important to run for office and pick your affiliation based on what you feel is right, not on whether or not it gives you the best chance of winning. You'll need to answer, not only to you family and your constituents after you're elected, but more importantly, to yourself.

In my county, I knew before I announced that the party I was choosing wasn't the one that was going to give me the best chance of winning. In my area, one party almost always wins all of the elections; but this wasn't the party I felt more closely aligned. I knew if I choose the other party just to win, I'd regret it.

Know your territory

Whether you're running for school board, alderman, mayor, county board member, state representative or one of any other seats available in your district, you'll need to know and understand your political boundaries. It won't do you any good if you go out and start campaigning if you're targeting people that can't even vote for you.

Township and district borders can be a little odd, zigging and zagging through neighborhoods, making even the most seasoned politician's head turn. In addition, about every decade, the political borders can change as territories re-district to balance the electorate.

Your best bet is to contact your board of elections and purchase a map of whatever district you're race is in.

It's usually a fairly small fee and you can often do it online, so there's no reason not to have a copy.

I purchased a poster-sized map and kept it pinned to my office wall from the moment I announced my candidacy to the very end; actually it's still hanging up on the wall right now. Whether you're going to go out canvassing a subdivision or you're invited to a neighborhood meet-and-greet, you'll be amazed how many times you'll need to reference the map and you'll be glad to have it so handy.

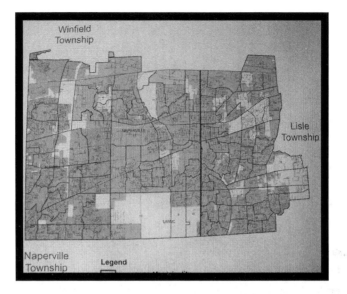

2010 DuPage County (IL) District 5 Map

This is the map from my race; DuPage (Illinois) County Board District 5. You'll notice that they break down more than just the county district. Within the county district, it is color coded for townships, cities, precincts and even unincorporated areas are broken out.

The district is a little different now than when I ran in 2010 due to the re-districting, so that just goes to show how things change. If you run for re-election, you'll most likely need to purchase a new territorial legend.

Your political future

Look to the future. What I mean is, think about *your* political future. Is this a one-time, one-office venture for you? Or do you want to make a career out of public life? If you're in it for the long-term, you may opt to make different choices and decisions about your political career.

For example, if you're solely running to change an unpopular citywide ordinance, you may decide a single run for mayor may be all you want. But if you have higher political aspirations and want to someday be governor, you may want to build with a couple terms on the city council followed by a run for mayor, on to a term or two as state senator, then to governor. These steps along the way will help you learn about the political process, make valuable connections and build a career.

Chapter 2

The Heart of the Campaign

Making Connections

I've briefly touched on how to start making the connections needed to run for office, but there's more to it than just making the call or sending an e-mail.

Prior to connecting, be prepared with answers to who, what, why and how of your plan. Your local party officials will want to know who you are. Not just your name, but what you've done. Like, do you have a political past or a criminal background? They'll ask about your employment, school history and what your family situation looks like. Questions like: Why are you running? How much time do you plan on devoting to winning? How do you plan on campaigning? How much money do you plan on spending? How do you think you'll raise the money? These are just a few questions you'll need to be prepared to answer.

Don't worry, if you're honest with a clean background and sincere intentions, you'll pass the test. Even if you don't have all the answers, a heartfelt approach should come across in your interview. If you're asked something to which you don't know the answer, ask for help and advice. In most cases, you're approach will be refreshing.

Ask for introductions to other political players in the area. Ask for advice on local fundraising. Ask for anything and everything. If they're willing to support you, they'll most certainly want you to win your race.

When I first met with the president of my county party, I asked who else I should talk to. I was given a list that included other party officers and county board members.

Within a week of that first meeting, I had lunch with an existing member of the county board. Tony Michelassi is a young, up-and-coming politician that took me under his wing and showed me how he won his race.

Sometimes I have a problem with people of authority who are younger than I am. And although I'm 15 years older than my political mentor, I didn't let ego get in the way of my learning. I sat and listened to everything he had to say. He talked about vote tally by precinct, breaking down which precinct leaned Democratic and which precinct usually voted Republican.

Prior to the meeting, I barely even knew what precincts were. After lunch, I was already targeting areas of the county that I should win, which areas I needed to avoid and which areas would be a battle.

This goes to show how important every little introduction and meeting can and should be. Use each opportunity to gather information for immediate and future use. The more you know about your area and the voters, the better your chances of victory.

I don't want to understate this point. Use the meetings, not just to meet influential people, but to gain the information they possess.

Along those same lines, this is the time you'll start attending, "meet the candidates," functions. Don't miss these. This is where you'll begin to pick up a little of the needed name recognition. In most cases, you'll have the opportunity to speak to the crowd, tell them who you are and why you want to be their representative. If it's a party-run event, you should use this time not just to explain who you are, but to begin the lobby for volunteers.

If you're anxious about public speaking, use these early opportunities to quell those feelings. It's early enough in the campaign that speaking stumbles won't adversely affect your standing in the public eye. So this is the perfect time to conquer the fear.

That fear can be debilitating and can affect your whole campaign. Work to get this out of the way early.

Later in the process you'll be involved in forums and debates; if you're nervous at a small luncheon, think about how you'll feel standing in front of a crowded auditorium.

Here are a few public speaking tips: take deep breaths and remain calm. Pick out a couple people in the audience and make eye contact – continue to look back and forth at these people making eye contact. This will give the impression that you're talking to everyone while connecting with different faces in the crowd. Remember that most of these people would be just as nervous as or more so than you are.

Just try and relax, the effort is half the battle – just get up there and do your best. The more you get in front of people and talk, the easier it gets.

Raising money

For most campaigns, you'll need to raise money. There's a lot involved in this process. There's not only the actual practice of raising money, but there's the paperwork that goes right along with it.

In smaller races, you don't always have the need for political funds. If you're town, county or district has very few people, you can likely pull off a successful campaign with no money just by personally getting your word out to everyone you know or run into.

But regardless of your race, I recommend raising at least a small amount of cash, just to cover the small expenses associated with campaigning.

There is an important thing to understand when raising money. Once you pass a certain threshold, you need to register your income with the state board of elections. You'll also need to file regular reports with the board to monitor campaign finance. Check with your local county or state board of elections for what and how to file your paperwork. In many cases, this can be done online.

The first time you file, what you'll actually be registering with the state is paperwork to form an official campaign committee.

When you raise money, the funds cannot be registered in your own name, there needs to be a committee with an objective to oversee the financials. The paperwork is submitted to your state and indicates your committee's goal. For me, the committee was, "Friends of Brian Duewel," and the objective was to elect Brian Duewel to the DuPage County Board.

You can opt for any of a number of options. You may choose something like, "Citizens to elect X." But whatever you choose, you'll have to have a treasurer to administer the account. If you choose, it can be the same as the candidate.

You'll also have to open a dedicated bank account in the committee's name. Again, for the sake of transparency, the money cannot sit in a personal account; it needs to be listed under the committee and the ledger needs to be filed with the state on a regular basis.

Just bring the registered paperwork into your local bank and tell them the type of account you're looking to open. They most likely know exactly what and how to fill out the forms to set-up your account.

Now, let's get to the actual fundraising. There are different ways to raise cash for your campaign. There's the direct ask. A phone call to a targeted list of potential donors is the most cost-effective, time-efficient way to build your bank. This list would include your family, friends, co-workers, past party donors, people who have similar dreams for your area and organizations with the same vision you have. Most of these people you'll call will be willing to donate a few dollars to your cause, if not because they agree with your politics, but because they like you.

Think about it like this, if you have a list of 100 people, and they each offer up $25, you already have a $2,500 bank. You didn't have to spend days planning a fundraiser, put up cash for a reception hall or sending out invitations. The direct ask is the best form of fundraising, and perhaps, it's all you'll need.

My golf fundraiser

If you need more, hold a fundraiser. For my race, I held two. I had a meet the candidate dinner and a summer golf outing. Both were successful - I raised a few thousand dollars at each event. They were a lot of work, but in the end, they were worth it.

One big key in planning a fundraiser is to recruit help. You don't need to be doing this alone; especially with all the other things you need to be worrying about during a campaign. Have someone scout locations, search for the best deal and send out invitations. All you should be doing is greeting people as they come in the door and accepting their gratitude, money and volunteerism.

How often you should be calling for donations and the number of and size of the fundraisers is determined by figuring out how much money you think you are going to need to successfully run your campaign.

How much money do you need?

Many new political hopefuls have no idea how much money they'll need to run for office. And to be honest, neither do I. The reason is, that it's all dependent on what office you're running for, the political landscape in your area, your personal standing in the community, the number of voters in your district, your opponent and his/her financial resources and a host of other issues.

Some things are easy to quantify; like your political landscape. If you know your town is overly Republican and you're planning to run as a Democrat, you'll need more money. And vise versa.

Also easy to quantify: your standing in the community. If you're a recognizable radio personality or car dealership owner, you might already have a little name recognition, but if you're a local accountant or tradesman, you'll need extra money to get your name out into the mainstream.

Quantifiable: number of voters. You can easily find out how many voters are in your district and how they voted in past elections, just check with your county board of elections; for a small fee, you can usually purchase this information.

As a general rule, the larger the office you're seeking, the more you'll want to raise. If you're running for small town alderman, you'll need less than if you're seeking the mayoral seat.

These are all things you can measure and prepare for accordingly. And the more things you can build a plan for, the better off your entire campaign will be because you'll know exactly where you stand all times.

But then there are the things you can't quantify, at least at certain times; like your opponent's budget. At different times, your opponent will be required to file financial reports, and then you can look to see their campaign balance. Until they do, you're flying blind. You also won't know how your opponent plans to spend their bank funds.

So as you can see, there are a number of variables at play when determining exactly how much money you'll need. Your best bet is to find a mentor who's been in your shoes. If you haven't already, talk to your political party and find out who's ran in the past and set up a meeting to find out what and how they ran their campaign, financially speaking.

Once you do that, you will have a much better grasp of exactly how much you'll need to win. The number may surprise you. It may be much less than you think, but it may also be a lot more than you anticipate.

When I had an early meeting with some local businessmen in my district, they told me to anticipate needing $100,000 to win my seat. I was blown away. I was thinking a couple thousand dollars. Knowing my circle of connections, I knew the number they were throwing out was a little unrealistic, but it was good to know.

End the end; I ended up raising around $8000. But I lost, so maybe those businessmen were right after all. The point is, talk to people who have been through the battle and see what they know. You may not be able to reach their goal, but at least you'll have a better grasp of what may be required.

Office Space

You'll need a dedicated location to call your campaign headquarters. For a small race, it may be the dining room table or your personal home office. For a larger campaign, you'll likely need to secure a place in an office building.

Either way, there's a couple things you need to have at your disposal. You'll need a phone, fax machine, copier, computer, printer, file cabinet, precinct maps, staplers, pens and pencils, mailing, walking and phone lists, envelopes, white out, note pads, clip boards, file folders and possibly much more.

If you have many volunteers helping around the clock, you'll probably have to get an office location. My advice: start small, and as you build your campaign fund, you'll be able to afford to move your headquarters to a local building (hopefully one where the manager supports your candidacy and offers you a price break on the rent or allows your signs out front).

Volunteers

Let's move on to topic of volunteers. You'll need them. If you plan on doing fundraisers, door-to-door campaigning and phone banking, you'll want the help. You should be out meeting people, not at golf courses looking for the best rates.

Volunteers are the lifeblood of a successful campaign. These are the people that want to help you win. In fact, it's their dream to see you succeed. So be sure to use every ounce of their generous volunteerism.

It can be a bit tricky when it comes to volunteers. They usually don't come to you offering 40 hours a week of their precious time. So you have to be cautiously optimistic when approaching potential helpers. My biggest tip: a potential volunteer is always just another emotional supporter until you *ask* for help.

Comb through your phone book, look at the donor list and pester your local party for names, then ask for help. But be specific. Tell your volunteers exactly what you want them to do. Don't leave the invitation open ended. More often than not, that ends up as an invitation to do nothing. If you want someone to walk door-to-door and hand out your literature, tell them exactly that. Once they offer help, come right out and say, "Thanks, I'd love your help, how about this Saturday. If you could walk your precinct and hand out these flyers, I'd really appreciate it."

If they were sincere in their offer to help, they'll be glad to oblige.

There are literally hundreds of jobs you can have your volunteers work on; use your imagination and use volunteers for everything. Here's a small list of possible volunteer positions: answering phones, making calls,

handing out flyers, data input, running errands, finding

sign locations, research the opponent, recruit other

volunteers, maintain and update the website, paint and

put up signs, host a meet-and-greet, organizing

information and taking pictures and video.

Small town campaigning & publicity

You'll find out early what kind of campaigning you'll be doing as you build you platform. For most small races, face-to-face contact will help build your name recognition. That means door-to-door canvassing and meet the candidate nights. It doesn't get more face-to-face than that.

Door-to-door canvassing is just as it sounds; you get a list of names from your party or board of elections, and walk from house to house meeting all the constituents in your town or district. This takes up a lot of your campaign time, actually, probably most of it, but this is where you win or lose. If you meet someone, shake their hand and listen to their concerns, you'll most likely get their vote.

The more people you meet, the more votes you get. So you need to do whatever you can to get out the vote. Walking in parades and attending festivals and fairs are also important face-to-face opportunities. Here's a perfect situation – participating at your political party's booth at the county fair. If you have the option of standing in one place, while all the perspective voters come to you, what more can you ask for in an afternoon of campaigning?

I used this opportunity to bring my son to help hand out my fliers. Even if someone feels like not being hassled by a politician, they're not likely to ignore a 7-year-old boy helping his dad.

My son Riley at the DuPage County Fair

The same philosophy holds true for parades. You get to walk a route that's already laid out for you, and meet everyone that's lined up to greet you. Make sure you don't just walk and waive. Take the time to stop and shake hands… remember my thought on a hand shake and a smile? It's worth a thousand votes – or at least the one you're shaking.

The only drawback to parades and fairs is that your opponent is most likely doing the exact same thing, thus negating your advantage. But if you do it better, you might persuade voters that weren't already there for you. Besides, if you don't do it, your opponent is gathering all the votes you're leaving behind.

Meet the candidate nights are set up so people interested in you or the election in general can come out and meet you, shake your hand and listen to your platform and ideas. Again, face-to-face contact builds a voter connection and that could mean the difference between winning and losing.

Signs and mailers are nice for name recognition, but nothing seals a voter choice like a hand shake and a smile. The great thing is that it's cheaper too.

But if you're area is large, you'll need to do more than just shake a few hands to win your election.

Personal phone calls and automated phone banking are helpful forms of campaigning. Phone lists can be found from either the county, usually for a small fee, or from your political party. Obviously, personal calls are more intimate and free, but automated calls reach more voters.

It may useful to use a combination of both. That's what I did. I personally called registered voters leading up to the election, and then the day before, I hired an automated call center to target thousands of voters.

There's also paid advertising materials like yard signs, parade hand-outs and mailers. There are hundreds of reputable outlets to purchase campaign materials. As soon as you file your paperwork for your campaign, you'll receive dozens of flyers in the mail offering services.

It's my experience that one service is about as good as another in this arena. I ordered from two separate dealers during my campaign and had a great experience both times.

I also used another form of marketing, sometimes referred to as "guerrilla marketing." I simply put up flyers with my message all around town. This is what the flyers, printed on an 8x12 sheet of paper looked like:

A friend drew up a design, I had a printing company mass produce a few hundred copies and a couple volunteers helped spread the word.

It wasn't a thousand dollar campaign or anything that I spent too much time on; I had an idea, asked a friend for help and that was about it.

Some of the best self-advertising comes in the form of radio and television interviews, debates and candidate forums.

In most cases, these will naturally find you. It's amazing how just having you name on a ballot can lead to publicity. A word of advice: act yourself, be honest and let the magic happen.

If you don't start getting invited to these events, ask your party officials for help. They'll know the people who are organizing these events and most likely have the pull to get you invited.

You can also take the publicity train in your own hands by writing a letter to the editor of your local paper. Talk about an issue that is important in your community and what'd you do about it. They won't always run your letter, but on occasion, they will – and that's targeted publicity.

If you have friends that are willing to write letters to the editor on your behalf, that's even better. That shows that someone cares enough about you and your platform to take the time to write a recommendation. I had a very generous friend do this for my campaign – and it did in fact run in the local paper.

You'll notice that much of the publicity you seek is free. Take full advantage of these forms of costless promotion.

As I searched for inexpensive advertising, I routinely came back to a relatively new form of media. It was with varying degrees of success that I used and loved social media.

In today's campaign times, you cannot look past this social tool. Almost everyone you know, and more importantly, everyone you want to vote for you, is on some sort of social medium. Whether it's Twitter, Facebook or LinkedIn, you have to jump on board if you're not already.

I actually used all three. I created a Twitter handle specifically for the campaign. Here I would tweet out political thoughts, stances, upcoming appearances, ideas, where to volunteer or give money, appreciation to supporters and positive advocacy thoughts. This Twitter channel was kept strictly campaign-professional and was never used for personal reasons.

On Facebook, I started a fan page where I would post updates and information on me, the candidate. You have to remember that people are searching for information on their candidates – you should be the one to put the info out there for them to find.

I used LinkedIn to post more updates and to target specific friends and connections for donations and support. On LinkedIn, I used my personal page.

At each of these places, I pasted my website URL and slogan everywhere. And speaking of website, if you didn't think you needed one – you're wrong.

Again, much like your Facebook page, you need to give the constituents a place to find information about you. Your site doesn't have to be complicated and cost thousands of dollars. It strictly needs to be a place to show your face, slogan and platform.

In the early days of my campaign, with the help of my volunteer campaign manager, we built our own page. It was modestly crude, but it provided everything I wanted. My political plan was there, my picture was there, my slogan was there and my contact info was there.

As the process moved on and I had a little money in the bank, I upgraded the site and made it look more professional. There are plenty of places to go for help in building a specialized site. Most of them allow you to pick a template at a low cost and you just plug in your information. The danger is that your opponent might inadvertently choose the same template.

There's a lot to learn and do, I know... but each of these steps help you build your name recognition. And, no pun intended, that's the name of the game.

If people don't know who you are, they won't vote for you. It's natural human instinct to align yourself with who you know. If they don't know you, you've lost their vote. Take every opportunity to gather every ounce of publicity you can.

In addition to social media and your own personal website, consider running an email campaign. As you meet people, gather their email addresses and give them regular campaign updates.

This is a great way to keep the electorate informed on your status. Give them your views, updates on issues, upcoming events, and volunteer opportunities along with other campaign notices.

You don't have to send individual emails to each person on your list, there are services available that can regulate your service. I've used a couple and I like 1ShoppingCart. Each email gets delivered as if it were mailed directly to the recipient, without showing the whole list to which the message is going out.

Feel free to shop around, but finding a single service to help automate your email process and take credit cards will greatly boost your efficiency.

Coming across as experienced

You could have all the publicity in the world, but if you appear clueless and uninformed, you'll likely lose.

Sometimes this may be more difficult than you might expect. It's not that you plan on going into a campaign event unprepared, but if you're up against an incumbent, he/she will automatically have the upper hand.

Incumbents will always have personal, hands-on, back-room information regarding whatever issue is hot. It's their job to know what's going on in the community. It's your job to learn what they know.

I made it a policy of my campaign to learn what my opponent knew, and when it seemed appropriate, took the opposing view. This helped me look knowledgeable, but with my own ideas on local issues.

I often listened to my rival, formed my own opinion on a topic and issued a press release stating my viewpoint and reasons for my opposition. Unfortunately, I didn't always gain traction with my press releases, but it's always worth the try. Besides, when a local reporter is always hearing your ideas, it makes you a much more viable candidate. Further on down the line, this should pay dividends with additional coverage on your candidacy.

Remember, the more often a reporter sees your name, hears your voice and listens to your ideas, the more coverage you'll receive.

If you haven't already, you should volunteer for service on a local board. It could be your PTA board or your community council, but whatever you decide, do it straight away. Even a small amount of experience on a board of directors shows leadership and expertise in governing. Don't underestimate this point, get some experience early. If you don't think there's anything you're qualified to do, think again. Look around your way of life – there are college reunion boards, industry association boards and plenty of non-profit board of director positions available all the time... these groups are always looking for help.

And speaking of help, volunteer your time. Clean the side of the road, feed the homeless, pitch-in at an animal shelter, pick up garbage at the forest preserve or bag food for the needy. If you want to help your community this is a great place to start. Call any non-profit in your area and ask how you can help; they'll be glad to have you.

People notice when their candidates are out doing good in the community, so get out there and volunteer. And while you're at it, take pictures and video and post it to your website. You should volunteer because you want to help others, but as someone who's looking to win an elected seat, you also need the voters to know what kind of person you are. Don't be ashamed to paparazzi yourself and post it, if people don't know about you, they won't vote for you.

This is what I did; my entire family spent one Saturday cleaning up at a forest preserve while my wife recorded the whole event on video and with pictures. Of all the times I have volunteered, I figured I'd let the voters see it once. I don't always flaunt my volunteerism, but every once in a while, as a candidate, it's necessary.

Political Functions

You may wonder what functions you need to attend, how to find out about them and when which are the most important.

My advice on this is actually pretty simple. Attend everything you can. Whether its debates, meet the candidate functions, press conferences, candidate forums or anything you're invited to, you need to make every attempt you can to go.

The more you're seen at these events, the more you're going to be noticed and come across as a legitimate candidate who's serious about the race. Go and talk to people, listen to their concerns and tell them how you plan on helping them. This is one of the best forms of campaigning, it's free and personal – two of the most important things in a small office race.

The best part is that you won't even have to do that much work to figure out where and when the events are happening, you'll be invited as soon as you register your candidacy. Some of the luncheons and meet-and-greets will be organized by you, your team or you're your party. But many of the functions, like debates and forums will be put on by different politically-minded organizations (like your local chamber of commerce or the League of Women's Voters).

Do your best to make all the functions, but if you can't make them all, some are more important than others. For example, you need to attend the debates and forums; these are the opportunities to go head-to-head with your opponent and differentiate yourself from his/her views.

Besides the obvious necessity of attending political functions for vote gathering, this is where you begin to create those political connections you were missing as you began your crusade. If an event is important to the voters in your district, you better bet it's important to other elected officials or notable businessmen.

By being there talking about who you are and what you stand for, you'll build those relationships that will help your campaign now and in the future.

You may not even realize it's even happening. You might be just talking to someone and he may say something like, "I own the business down the street, I'd love to have your signs in our windows." Or maybe you're in a conversation and you hear, "Do you know the Governor? I'd love to introduce you." And boom; now you have your connections.

That's about what happened to me a number of times. I got the chance to meet, talk to and learn from my Governor, U.S. Senator and a couple of congressmen.

U.S. Senator Dick Durbin

Illinois Governor Pat Quinn

U.S. Congressman Bill Foster

A lot of it may seem like just name-dropping, but in a sense, that's what politics is all about; who you know. And remember, you probably didn't have any "who you knows," when you started this whole process.

Endorsements

There are countless reasons to want to know important people in the political world. One of the more important is the chance to get their endorsement.

A single endorsement probably won't win you the election; but people listen to people they know and like. So if you're running for mayor and you have no name recognition, it would be quite beneficial to your campaign if the sitting governor says how great you are.

Think about how awesome it would be if the governor, senator and a representative all sang your praises.

Now, not only are you a person who has political connections, but you become one of the "it" people that others look to for advice and guidance.

Your Look

If you don't already have it, get yourself a nice headshot (photograph of your face) or two. It doesn't have to be professionally done, but it should be a clean, crisp, high quality .jpg. Don't take a shot where you're cropping someone out of the picture; set aside some time, dress sharp and have someone snap a couple shots. Make sure the lighting is good and the background is clean; and just like that, you have a political headshot available to whoever wants one.

You'll be surprised how often a newspaper, website or organization will request a headshot of you, the candidate.

If you have it ready to send at an instant's notice, you won't waste a whole lot of time rushing around trying to dress, get a camera and a photographer to snap a shot so you can send it to your local paper. When you

receive a request, simply click and send.

Questionnaires

Quite often during the process, you'll receive surveys, or questionnaires in the mail asking for your views on different issues. These are usually issued by organizations or PAC's (political action committees). An example of an organization that would send a questionnaire is the League of Women's Voters and an example of a PAC would be Personal PAC. There are hundreds of organizations, unions and PAC's that are looking for answers from candidates and often are looking to endorse a candidate. Sometimes you'll know immediately if you're answering the questions the way they want, or if you're obviously not the intended endorsee.

For example, if you favor strict gun control and the NRA (National Rifle Association) sends you a questionnaire, you should know right off that you're not who they're looking to endorse.

Answer the survey anyway, with honest responses. You're always better off replying than looking like you don't even care. Besides, they might post your answers somewhere that everyone can see it; and if you answers strike a chord with a couple like-minded readers, you'll pick up a couple votes. The people that weren't going to vote for you anyway still probably won't, but answering the questionnaire didn't change that.

Polls

Here's my thought on polls... although they are more than helpful, in a local election, I'd avoid paying for them. Polls can be costly and they can blow your whole budget. Most times, you'll instinctively know where you stand anyway just because you have an intimate knowledge of your district.

If your party or another local candidate is paying for the information, that's even better. Use the knowledge to your advantage by understanding your precincts and where the need for persistent campaign pressure is located.

If you're running for a larger office, like state senate or state representative, you're going to have to cough up the dough to have polling done. In races of this size (and larger) you're going to need to know where you stand at all times. You need to know if you need to dial up the fundraising, volunteer work and overall campaigning.

Contact your local party organization to figure out exactly who they use to do the local polling and contact them directly. Most likely in a race of this size (state senate or state representative), you'll have a professional campaign manager anyway, so make them do this for you; after all, it's their job.

Tip: If there's other local candidates in the same boat as you are, see if you can pool your money together for one large polling campaign.

Chapter 3

Avoid burnout

Life outside the campaign

Your time as a candidate will be all consuming. You'll eat, sleep and drink the campaign.

During my time as a candidate, I consistently was thinking about what I should be doing. I was constantly worried that I wasn't working hard enough. I always thought about what additional steps I could make to further my chances.

The problem? Half way through my campaign, I began to burn out. I started to get sick and I was totally rundown. Even in my free time, I wasn't free.

I needed to make a change, or I wasn't going to make it to the election in one healthy piece.

I decided to take a vacation... right in the middle of the campaign. It may not be advisable from a campaign manager's point of view, but it's what I needed to do. And I recommend, if you have too much anxiety or extreme fatigue, take a break from it all and get away.

Sometimes all it takes is a weekend to recharge the batteries.

Involve your family

It should go without saying, but you want to have the family involved. From the initial decision making process to the actual campaign, keeping the family in the loop will make the whole process more rewarding.

Things like, family support at parades and fairs, a significant other supporting you at a debate, or parents and children handing out flyers, not only means a lot personally and emotionally, but the extra help is practically immeasurable.

Some of my best memories are going door-to-door with my 7-year-old son. I didn't force or even ask him to walk with me; it was something he just wanted to do with his dad. He saw at an early age how important the election was to me and he wanted to be there to support his daddy.

That meant more to me than almost anything throughout the campaign.

Chapter 4

Just Do It

Your team

So once you've made the decision, it's time to get moving. That means, build your team, get your paperwork in, develop your slogans and plan your attack.

When it's time to gather your help, start by recruiting, or hiring if you have the means, a campaign manager. My friend Zach Bambacht offered to be my volunteer manager. Together we plotted my meetings, appearances, speeches and endorsements.

Depending on the size of office you're seeking, you may need to actually pay a professional to be your manager. There's a lot that goes into this job. They have to make sure you're prepared for your appearances and interviews, they set up your events and meetings, they work to deflect any unwanted conflict and they handle most of your paperwork and requests.

Most smaller campaigns don't have a paid campaign manager, but if you can, do. If you cannot, do what I did and recruit a friend to take on the responsibility. But look for someone who's dedicated to your cause because this can be a stressful, time-consuming job.

If you're taking on both candidate and campaign manager (and more than likely, treasurer) roles on your own, be ready for a ton of work and plenty of aggravation. Each position is intense on its own, but when you're doing both, if you really plan on doing both simultaneously; it's going to be absolutely all consuming.

Even if you can get a little assistance to ease the load as you prepare your events, statements and paperwork, you'll get through the whole process much easier. And who should you ask for the help? Just look towards your volunteer base; someone there should be able to pitch in and help pick up some of the workload.

As I mentioned earlier, volunteers are the lifeblood to any campaign, so I called friends, neighbors and family and asked for help. A couple dozen people offered up their services at different events on my behalf. Those that couldn't help physically, donated financially to the cause.

From parades, phone banking and door-to-door campaigning, there's just too much to do alone. The more volunteers you have, the more your name and message are out there attracting voters.

With the financial assistance you receive, start building your message. Signs, handouts, mailers, shirts, car magnets, business cards and pins are just a few of the hundreds of campaign items you can use to build your name recognition. I urge you and your team to look through and decide what you want, what you need and what you can afford. Weigh the costs from different companies and proceed with your best interests in mind.

Personally, I picked up yard signs, door hangers, shirts, business cards, pencils and post-it notes. I placed the signs around the county and hung the door hangers with my information as I went door-to-door around my district. The cards, pencils and notes were handed out at outings and parades by everyone wearing my shirts.

The decision of what exactly you need is somewhat personal and depends on your voters. I feel that almost every candidate needs a minimum of some kind of yard signs. I know some people disagree with this, but if people see your name everywhere they turn, you'll build name recognition. I've heard people say,

"Signs don't translate into votes," but I believe that from a cost benefit, they help enough to make it a necessity.

Whether you buy them or make them, just get some and pass them out. Ask friends, neighbors and supporters to place them in their yards. Watch where other candidates place their signs; often candidates place signs on vacant corners and empty parkways, so if everyone else is doing that, do it too.

Visit local businesses and ask if you can put your sign in the window or on their lawn. People that visit those establishments will see and notice your name.

Once the election is over, win or lose, you need to go and pick up your yard signs. Many towns and districts will fine you if your material stays out for too long after Election Day.

There are different opinions on what to put on your sign. Some people think your name and the office you're seeking is good, while others think you need to put, "vote," "elect" or "re-elect" on the sign. I've seen donkeys (for democrats), elephants (for republicans), trees (running for forest preserve), gavels (running for judge) and countless other designs. I notice signs with black, red, yellow, blue, green, and all other colors.

Here's my thought – try to keep it simple and easy to read. I had a friend that was running for office one time and used yellow for the signs. When you were driving by, the color didn't pop and you couldn't read what the message was.

I believe bold, dark colors work better than bland or hard to read colors. I used a deep, dark blue and red on a white background. Actually, all I did was have my slogan placed on my signs; simple, concise and easy to read.

I actually placed my slogan on all my merchandise so everyone knew who I was and what I was running for. That leads me to something that's often overlooked, yet I think is critical to elected success.

Slogans

A great slogan or logo won't necessarily win you the election, but it will help brand your identity and build name recognition. For me it was "Duewel for DuPage."

I chose this for obvious reasons, my name is Brian Duewel and I was running for a seat on the DuPage County Board. It was short, sweet and easy to remember. Anyone who saw my slogan immediately knew my name and what I was running for.

I branded everything with it. The pencils and notes that were handed out said, "Duewel for DuPage." The shirts everyone wore said, "Duewel for DuPage." The car magnets said, "Duewel for DuPage." I wanted to make sure everyone always connect the two.

When voters were at home taking notes, I wanted them to think about me and my campaign. When kids were doing their homework with my pencils, I wanted

the parents to think about me and my campaign. I think

you get my point – it's all about name recognition.

Tell everybody

Once you build your platform, tell everybody. And I mean everybody.

At the store, at the library, at your kid's school and at the restaurant, make sure everybody knows who you are and what you're doing. Again, it's about building your message and name recognition.

Most people you meet will be more than happy to say hello and ask about your campaign. Use this to connect to your constituents.

It's actually pretty simple, just walk up, introduce yourself and explain what you're doing. "Hello, my name is Brian Duewel; I'm running for a seat on the DuPage County Board. I just want to take a moment to introduce myself." Then launch into regular conversation. More often than not, you'll end up with a nice talk. Every once in a while, you'll get someone that wants nothing to do with you, your stance or politics in general, simply thank them for their time and move on.

Election Day

So you've made it all the way to Election Day. Congratulations.

But your work isn't over. This is the "day of days" for your campaign, so there's still a lot of work to be done.

On this day, you'll need plenty of volunteers and you'll need to have a plan. Have the volunteers head out to polling locations with literature to hand out to voters (just be sure to instruct them about local voting ordinances – you have to stay away from the actual doors of the polling center).

Have another set of volunteers make calls to all registered party voters in your town to remind them how important their vote is to get you elected. Each volunteer should get a set of numbers and call all morning and afternoon.

Do everything you can to get the vote out, so do your best to call every registered party member in your district and get them to the polls. Even if that means having someone actually go and physically drive them to the polls. Remember, every vote counts in small town elections.

Oh yeah, don't forget to vote yourself.

Then go out for a nice meal with your family and go watch the results come in at your election night victory party.

Part 2
Other candidates experiences, views and thoughts

This is the part of the book where I felt it necessary to recruit information from others who have walked the walk.

As much as I learned during my run, I realized there was more I wanted to know.

I decided I wanted to gather advice from candidates that have actually won an election. I wanted to know what experiences they went through, what advice was given to them and what they learned from the process.

I sent out questionnaires to thousands of elected officials from all around the country, from city council members and mayors to state senators and county board commissioners. I tried to focus more on the smaller, local offices, primarily because that's who this book is meant to guide.

I offered local politicians the chance to answer one of six questions about their experience in their first race. Aside from minor grammatical fixes and slight factual changes, I left their answers as they responded. I thought it was important to hear their answers in their voice.

The questions or comments they were to choose from included:

Tell a funny story or anecdote from the campaign trail.

What advice did someone else give you that helped you through your first campaign?

What's the biggest piece of advice you have for a political newbie?

What did you learn as you were running your first campaign?

How should someone go about raising money, name awareness, or making political connections?

How did you win your election?

Often, the candidates answered several of the questions. In these cases, I picked just one of the answers. I did this for several reasons. First, I didn't want just a couple candidates to dominate the entire book. Second, I wanted a sense of consistency throughout the guide, and if each official was allotted one answer, this seemed to accomplish that goal.

Within their single entry, some officials gave me a one sentence answer while others went on for multiple pages. Again, with the answer, I tried to include it verbatim, they way they intended.

Other than the first entry, the following is in no particular order. I don't know or care how many Republicans or Democrats are listed or in what order. This is a book about running for office with no money, name recognition or connections, not about politics. In fact, I actually only know the political party of one participant. And that's the first person listed in the book. The first elected official was picked to be first for a specific reason: John Zediker is the man who defeated me in my race. I figured what better way to show no bias than to put my own opponent first.

John Zediker

Office:

County Board Member

Where:

DuPage County, Illinois

Elected to this office:

2010

First elected to any office:

2010

First run for office:

2010

What did you learn as you ran your first campaign?

"Like most first-time candidates, I paid my fair share of 'dumb dues' in my first race. I spent money on the wrong things and I tried to do too much with too little. Aside from the operational lessons, perhaps the greatest 'take-away' was to keep things in perspective. We have all seen the obnoxious parent at the youth soccer game that embarrasses themselves (and their kids) by making a scene when protesting a referee's call or the professional golfer who misses a putt for the championship and develops an incurable case of the yip. We say to ourselves 'what were they thinking' or don't they realize that 'it is just a game.' Well, like the parent or the golfer who get caught up in the moment and can't let it go - don't be the political version of that guy!!!

Politics can be a blood-sport if you allow it to be. In the heat of battle, we can get wrapped up in who said what to whom, who stole your campaign sign from the neighbor's yard, who did or didn't endorse you, or the 'betrayal' of a friend who supports your opponent. Don't get me wrong, all of these things bother the heck out of me too, but I (with the constant reinforcement from my family and friends) decided to not be that guy, and try the best I can to check the wild emotion, the irrational fear, and the unnecessary anxiety at the door that come with a spirited campaign. It is sometimes easier said than done!

"I will be the first to admit, I don't like to lose any more than the next guy. But I have seen and heard the horror stories of how campaigns have ruined relationships, careers, and put people into long periods of despair. At the end of the day, while public service is extremely important, it too needs to be kept in its proper perspective. The results of a local election should never define who you are and if it does then you are in public service for the wrong reason.

"If you keep things in their proper perspective, then win, lose, or draw, a campaign and (hopefully) serving out your term will be rich and rewarding experiences. If you don't - it is going to be a long campaign season (and if you win - a long couple of years) for you, your family and friends!!"

Annise D. Parker

Office:

Mayor

Where:

Houston, Texas

Elected to this office:

_2010_

First elected to any office:

_1998_

First run for office:

_1991_

How to raise money/name awareness/make political connections:

"Raising money is one of the things I most dislike doing but you can't run a campaign without money. I hate 'call time' and have been known to procrastinate leaving my city office for my campaign office. But raise money you must, with the emphasis on you. Take a deep breath; sit at the phone with a list supplied you by your campaign finance staff and call one person after another. Be tenacious. Hire an experienced finance director who can put together good donor lists.

"The best way to raise name awareness is to be active in the community—through organizational leadership and neighborhood work and, actually, working for other candidates.

"You <u>make political connections</u> by working in political campaigns and political parties as a volunteer. Identify the behind-the-scenes political activists and powers-behind-the-throne in your community and visit with them before you ever announce your candidacy."

Mark W. Klingensmith

Office:

Mayor

Where:

Sewall's Point, Florida

Elected to this office:

2010

First elected to any office:

2008

First run for office:

2008

How to raise money/name awareness/make political connections:

"Creating name awareness facilitates developing connections. Making connections then enables fundraising. Therefore, at the start, the first thing you should do is to create name awareness.

"Actually, this is easier than it may sound. Opportunities to create name awareness come in many forms. Call the editor of your local newspaper and request the opportunity to write a guest column on a particular issue; volunteer on a local political campaign; join your local political committee, and volunteer to chair a function or activity. Creating name awareness does not have to be, at the outset, name awareness throughout the general community. It might start out as name awareness among the movers and shakers of the local political scene.

"If you create a reputation as an active member of your local political community, you'll attract the attention of current officeholders. Also, you may consider running for office first within your local political committee to allow you to experience running an election, albeit on a somewhat smaller scale rather than jumping in to a county-wide race for your first try. By successfully running for local party office, this will allow you to work on a daily basis with community elected officials on various initiatives, and perhaps lead to being asked to become involved in their re-election campaigns.

"Working on an officeholder's re-election campaign will create name awareness with local political campaign contributors such that you can develop

personal relationships with them, gain their trust, and

thus enable you to successfully fund-raise from those

sources."

Sandy Nolte

Office:

City Council (Dist. 4)

Where:

New Braunfels, Texas

Elected to this office:

2009

First elected to any office:

2009

First run for office:

2009

What's the biggest piece of advice you'd give a political newbie?

"Be prepared to have someone run against you up until the end would be my best advice."

Shelley Welsch

Office:

Mayor

Where:

University City, Missouri

Elected to this office:

_2010_

First elected to any office:

_2002_

First run for office:

_2002_

What's the biggest piece of advice you'd give a political newbie?

"The most important piece of advice I would give to someone who is considering running for public office would be to be sure they are running for the right reason. Today, like it or not, politics has become a high-profile, "movie star" field. Too many people enter politics because they want to be known; they want to see their name in print and their face on television, and hear their voice on the radio. They appear to be in politics for themselves, and for the prestige that is sometimes connected with the job. I would tell a newcomer to be sure his/her interest is based in a desire to serve; to work for their neighbors; to listen to their concerns; and to do the work necessary to deal with them. If public service is not at the base of your desire to run, you should not run.

"Running a campaign is about making personal contacts. It's about going door-to-door as much as possible (if you are running in a race where the size of a district makes that doable); it's about asking your family, friends and neighbors to give money at the start to kick-off a campaign; it's about taking the time to sit down with people in your community who can provide insight into their neighborhoods, organizations, businesses and communities; it's about volunteering in your community and attending meetings prior to a campaign so you know the issues, and so should know why you are running; it's about learning to build a budget so that you can reach the voters in as many ways as possible; and it's about having the courage to ask people you don't know to support you with their financial contributions, and being able to assure them their funds will be well used.

"In my first campaign, I was encouraged to run by a neighbor, Harriett Woods, who had been a Senator in the State of Missouri; had been the Lieutenant Governor of our state; and who twice served as president of the National Women's Political Caucus. She reminded me that this was MY campaign. I had to be willing to walk the streets to get the signatures on my nominating petition; I had to be willing to canvass door to door in lovely and lousy weather; I had to be willing to do whatever I would ask volunteers to do on my behalf.

"The other side of this was that I had to be willing to fight for my campaign. When volunteers came on to help, giving lots of their time to the cause, and giving lots of advice on what I should be saying or how I should be conducting the campaign, I had to be able to retain control. A candidate needs to know how to put a campaign together and be willing to ask for and accept help, but the candidate cannot lost track of who he or she is, and the candidate must stay true to the reason for running – and not let the heady feeling you might feel as a candidate get in the way of sticking to your principles.

"Remember, this is not personal. As a candidate you can't take all criticism to heart, you can't allow your feelings to be hurt. And you can't and should not come to believe the campaign is about you, personally. It's about you, as someone who wants to serve the public, being lucky enough to have others consider you for that special job.

"Never forget who put you in office if you win. And if you lose, try again."

S. Scott Vandergrift

Office:

Mayor

Where:

Ocoee, Florida

Elected to this office:

1992

First elected to any office:

1967

First run for office:

1967

What funny story or anecdote do you have from the campaign trail?

"One lady said she voted for me because she saw the other candidate pick his nose in public."

"I am an environmentalist and we hand paint our campaign signs. We use a lot of symbols such as trees and school houses to make a point. We put on one sign that I was a tree hugger and a lady called and wanted to know what that meant. I told her we didn't know how to spell environmentalist. She laughed and got the point."

Kathy DeRosa

Office:

Mayor

Where:

Cathedral City, California

Elected to this office:

2004

First elected to any office:

1998

First run for office:

1998

What funny story or anecdote do you have from the campaign trail?

"My first run for Mayor was against an incumbent who had 50 times more money they I had and as is said in politics, he had no "fatal flaws". I explained to my campaign committee we would launch a grassroots campaign as there was no way we would or could spend $100,000. I borrowed a friend's big red pickup truck, outfitted it with a speaker system and began driving through the community with my message blasting everywhere while handing out pens with my name on it and speaking with people who came out to see what was going on. It was so much fun. Election night was a cliff hanger. I was losing all night and at 11:00 pm, we finally learned we were ahead by 62 votes. When the election was certified, we won by 121 votes that first time. I am now serving my 4th term."

M. Jane Seeman

Office:

Mayor

Where:

Vienna, Virginia

Elected to this office:

2000

First elected to any office:

1992

First run for office:

1992

What advice did someone else give you that helped you through your first campaign?

"On raising money… we don't. We finance our own campaigns so we reuse signs from the previous campaign. You don't put 'elect' because then the following years you have to get a new sign that says 'reelect'. Our residents are suspicious of anyone spending too much. One year someone did a phone survey and boy did I get questioned about that even though it didn't cost me anything."

Ira Bowman

Office:

Mayor

Where:

Wilton, Iowa

Elected to this office:

_2009_

First elected to any office:

_2007_

First run for office:

_2009_

What's the biggest piece of advice you'd give a political newbie?

"The one thing I told people from the very beginning was 'I may not always agree with you but I will always listen to you.' That's a promise I have kept. I think people have responded to that. My advice is hear people out before responding especially if you don't agree with them. They may change your mind."

Sharon Goldsworthy

Office:

Mayor

Where:

Germantown, Tennessee

Elected to this office:

1994

First elected to any office:

1994

First run for office:

1994

What's the biggest piece of advice you'd give a political newbie?

"Form a small, compatible committee of committed supporters who will tell you what you need to hear, not what you'd like to hear. Present yourself as a person who may be willing to compromise on issues but never on values. Many constituents tell you what they want. Discern what they actually need. There's a difference. When you focus on the underlying need, you may be able to offer more, different or better options than what they ask or demand."

Tom Hansen

Office:

State Senator

Where:

Nebraska (Dist. 42)

Elected to this office:

_2004_

First elected to any office:

_2004_

First run for office:

_2004_

What did you learn as you ran your first campaign?

"The entire campaign was a learning process. People gave me their views on every subject under the sun. Some were national issues that are not under the state's control. Some were not on my radar but still showed up there. I tried not to explain my position but rather listened to the concerns of those who ended up as my constituents. Through those conversations over several months people got comfortable with me and I got surer of what was going to be expected of me if elected. Being elected is a sincere honor and a responsibility to stay in contact with the folks at home. That is why I go home every weekend to make that connection. The education goes on. The issues change and the contacts continue to grow with the e-news letter that goes out every two weeks from my Legislative office. My young

opponent ended up running and was elected to be Mayor

of our town. We all learn from life's experiences!"

Donnalee Lozeau

Office:

Mayor

Where:

Nashua, New Hampshire

Elected to this office:

2008

First elected to any office:

1984

First run for office:

1984

What advice did someone else give you that helped you through your first campaign?

"At the age of 24, I successfully ran for state representative from my ward in the second largest city of the state after having a discussion with a state representative from a nearby town. She advised me that if I wasn't happy about the way I thought 'politicians' did their jobs, which seemed to me was that they always just told you what they thought you wanted to hear not what you needed to know, that I needed to get involved, not just complain. She knew it was very effective to make change from the inside out.

"Get involved. I did. I went door to door in my ward and introduced myself and listened to what the concerns were of the neighborhood. I openly and directly shared my beliefs and concerns. Most importantly, I let each person know that I understood that if elected I would be representing them and would be available and welcome their comments and insight."

Rick Taylor

Office:

Committeeman

Where:

Pennsauken, New Jersey

Elected to this office:

1995

First elected to any office:

1995

First run for office:

1995

What advice did someone else give you that helped you through your first campaign?

"I always kept in mind something that a good friend had given to me as advice when I was beginning my career as an elected official, he said 'Rick, you can't have rabbit ears... you have to keep a thick skin or you will never survive.' I continue to remind myself of that when on the occasions I have been criticized and keep in mind that I don't have all the answers. I have also learned that you can do 100 things for somebody but sometimes they only remember the one thing you couldn't do. It all comes back to believing in yourself and doing your job to the best of your ability and with the best of intentions."

Gary Fuller

Office:

Mayor

Where:

Opelika, Alabama

Elected to this office:

_2004_

First elected to any office:

_2000_

First run for office:

_2000_

What's the biggest piece of advice you'd give a political newbie?

"Be careful what you ask for. Make sure you want the job or position you are running for. Get in the race early and outwork your opponents. Radio, newspaper, direct mail, billboards, tee-shirts… all great ways to advertise, but it's hard to beat going door-to-door asking folks up close and personal for their vote."

W. Suzanne Handshoe

Office:

Mayor

Where:

Kendallville, Indiana

Elected to this office:

2003

First elected to any office:

2003

First run for office:

1999

Did you raise money for your campaign?

"One must go into the first campaign with the idea that there may not be any financial resources. Host an old fashioned BBQ or ask ladies from different circles, church groups or even small neighborhood coffee's to get to know you and make a donation if they feel compelled."

Bill Swintkowski

Office:

Mayor

Where:

Hayward, Wisconsin

Elected to this office:

_2009_

First elected to any office:

_1987_

First run for office:

_1987_

What did you learn as you ran your first campaign?

"One thing I did learn when I ran for Mayor the first time is never underestimate the power of Social Media. That was the time when everyone was clamoring for change whether it be right, wrong or indifferent. We were also in the midst of a Presidential election. I was aware of Facebook and those sorts, but never gave it a second thought. Well, lo and behold I darn near lost that election and it was all because of Facebook. Unfortunately I found out about it after the fact, but all still turned out well."

Doug Pierce

Office:

Mayor

Where:

Norwalk, Iowa

Elected to this office:

2009

First elected to any office:

2009

First run for office:

2009

What's the biggest piece of advice you'd give a political newbie?

"I agreed to run because key leadership within the City of Norwalk talked to me and asked me to do so because of my 39 years of military leadership experience. When I said yes, I felt that the incumbent would be reelected, so the point is, if you decide to run, know that you can win and be ready for that responsibility. Once I made the decision to run, then you need to find a person(s) who have experience in running campaigns, especially if you are a "newbie". That helped me considerably to start the fund raising, letter writing, newspaper ads/articles and yard sign design. Because my military career was in the Air Force, I had blue background (Air Force service color) signs with two stars on them (I retired as a two-star general) and had an F-16 in a climbing attitude (I flew the F-16 for 10 years) to reflect a positive sense things getting better – the yard signs reflected my military career. My newspaper articles/ads and letters that were mailed to all the listed voters in Norwalk reflected on my years of military discipline, leadership capabilities, experience and financial management responsibilities as a Commander of over 2200 members."

Scott Mangold

Office:

Mayor

Where:

Powell, Wyoming

Elected to this office:

2004

First elected to any office:

2004

First run for office:

2004

What did you learn as you ran your first campaign?

"During my first campaign, I mentioned that the City of Powell would have a hard time paying for a new swimming pool on its own. The newspaper article said that I was against a swimming pool. Soon, I was labeled, 'anti-pool' which soon translated to 'he hates children.' I learned a lesson on that issue. Always try to put a positive spin or positive outcome on a situation. I helped campaign for a new aquatic center after that so I no longer hated children."

Bucky Johnson

Office:

Mayor

Where:

Norcross, Georgia

Elected to this office:

2008

First elected to any office:

2008

First run for office:

2008

What did you learn as you ran your first campaign?

"I did a website which had a video which began at our house and then was shot throughout the city. I did a number of coffees and appearances and then made about 750 personal phone calls. Most of the calls went to an answering machine so I would use their name on the message so that they knew it was not a robo call and it made it personal. Closer to the election, I did yard signs and house-to-house visits concentrating on the regular voters only. I did not send out one piece to the entire voter list. The Sunday before general election, I had many friends and committee members at my house making phone calls on my behalf. If someone had a question or comment, they handed their cell phone to me to talk to the citizen. The day of the election, I stood on a corner near the voting site with my campaign sign all day. My wife and other supporters stood with throughout the day. In the general election, Lillian got a few more votes than I did but we faced each other in a runoff. I did similar campaigning in the runoff and defeated her with about 60% of the vote. Since then I have been reelected once with no opposition and I am up again this fall (we have two year terms).

"What I learned is that hard work and a personal grass roots approach and hard work paid off. I won the campaign without attacking my opponents but talking about my vision for the city. I had no experience running for any office any I faced a veteran incumbent that spent twice as much as I did and used a political consultant."

Wayne Silas

Office:

Mayor

Where:

Winfield, Alabama

Elected to this office:

_2008_

First elected to any office:

_2008_

First run for office:

_2008_

How did you raise money/name awareness/make political connections?

"I never had to raise money but I have found if someone wants to give you money, there are strings attached. My advice is to stay clear of that.

"While I was in a restaurant once, I observed a local attorney who was a great politician going around to each table, greeting everyone. I've used this method myself many times over and have found it works. Friends however, are your best political connections."

<u>*Tony Petelos*</u>

Office:

County Manager

Where:

Jefferson County, Alabama

Elected to this office:

2011

First elected to any office:

1986

First run for office:

1986

How did you raise money/raise name awareness/make political connections?

"Get involved in charitable organizations; make a difference in your community; work outside your comfort zone; make new friends; volunteer to work on political campaigns whether it's a local election, gubernatorial or presidential"

Suzanne Atwell

Office:

**Mayor**

Where:

**Sarasota, Florida**

Elected to this office:

_**2011**_

First elected to any office:

_**2009**_

First run for office:

_**2005**_

What's the biggest piece of advice you'd give a political newbie?

"It really takes a mixture of skills to run effectively: One can know the issues inside and out, but you must translate that to the electorate in a way that they hopefully: like you, trust you, and feel you care about them. Having an outgoing personality is important. The effectiveness of the message on whatever issue, rests with how you engage with your constituents.

"I first ran for City Commission in 2005 and lost, but fared pretty well considering this was my first entre into politics. I was building my reputation and sometimes it takes a loss—not to feel defeated, but empowered to go for it again. Four years later, 2009, I ran again, and won in a runoff…

"I think what put me over the edge in my campaign was my dogged commitment to going door to door. It was exhausting, but critical to come face to face with my constituents (I was running At-Large which constitutes the entire purview of the City rather than a particular district). I can't emphasize enough the importance of this. Even those who may disagree with you will remember you took the time to come to their home and engage with them."

Donnie Henriques

Office:

Mayor

Where:

Woodstock, Georgia

Elected to this office:

_2005_

First elected to any office:

_1999_

First run for office:

_1999_

How did you raise money for your campaign?

"Raising money is best done on a small scale for a small town. Neighborhood meet and greets, where people donate small amounts from $10 up to $100 was how my first campaign was funded. I was recruited to run by the then Mayor for a new Council seat, so he introduced me to many people who could help me, both with votes and money."

Brian Landers

Office:

Mayor

Where:

Wisconsin Dells, WI

Elected to this office:

2011

First elected to any office:

2006

First run for office:

2006

What did you learn as you were running your first campaign?

"Do your research. Know your opponents, especially their weakness, but never sling mud at them. Use facts and issues that strike a chord with the community and don't just point them out....but bring solutions and a plan to the table to address them. In my run for Mayor of Wisconsin Dells, I faced a very popular 2 term incumbent who had a lot of business ties. I entered the race as a former police officer from the community who listened to the citizens who felt neglected by our leadership in favor of supporting businesses. I developed a slogan called "Community F.I.R.S.T. (Finances, Infrastructure, Residential growth, Schools, and Tourism) and had a plan to improve upon each one. I did tons of research on every issue and I went door to door

campaigning on how I would improve their

neighborhoods and businesses based upon the FIRST

theory and plan I developed. I am now in the process of

carrying out this plan of improvement as the newly-

elected Mayor, which was a result of the research I did

prior to the campaign."

George Scherck

Office:

Mayor

Where:

Neenah, Wisconsin

Elected to this office:

2002

First elected to any office:

1974

First run for office:

1974

What's the biggest piece of advice you'd give a political newbie?

"My advice for anyone running for political office is simple-become well known and respected in your community. I taught and coached for 32 years, attended almost every community event, volunteered for a variety of activities thus becoming well known in the community providing a solid basis for raising funds and gaining political support. What I learned in politics was to be myself, not only as a candidate but as Mayor. If you 'walk the walk' people will respect you and continue to support you in your career."

Leonard Urban

Office:

Mayor

Where:

Connersville, Indiana

Elected to this office:

_2008_

First elected to any office:

_1968_

First run for office:

_1968_

What funny story or anecdote do you have the campaign trail?

"One of the greatest stories I always remember was in 1968 in a poor area of our town on a cold October evening. There was a man working underneath a mobile home. I got down on all fours to hand him a card. He growled and said, 'I'm not interested' so, I rolled over on my back and reached up to help him do what he was doing. As he finished, I started to roll out from under the trailer. He said, 'hey son, give me one of those cards.' I have never forgotten how he became a friend."

Brian Grim

Office:

Mayor

Where:

Cumberland, Maryland

Elected to this office:

_2010_

First elected to any office:

_2008_

First run for office:

_2006_

**What's the biggest piece of advice you'd give a
political newbie?**

"A successful campaign requires two things:

1) Name recognition

2) Money

"Earning them is what much of the political
campaign process is all about. One can be a tool for
getting the other, but without either, victories are rare.
The key to both is to plan, organize, and give yourself
plenty of time. I made one big mistake in my campaign
for office. I waited too long to announce my candidacy
and begin fundraising. That's the first piece of advice I'd
give any potential candidate – start early. No matter
what amount of time you think you need or what amount

of money you think you'll spend, you always need more!"

Tommy Allegood

Office:

Mayor

Where:

Acworth, Georgia

Elected to this office:

2000

First elected to any office:

1998

First run for office:

1998

What's the biggest piece of advice you'd give a political newbie?

"Make sure you develop your own personal vision and message designed to make life better for everyone in your community, city, county and state. And then every day that you serve, make sure you consistently tell everyone why the message can, or is, making a difference in their life."

Earl Jaques, Jr.

Office:

State Representative

Where:

Delaware (Dist. 27)

Elected to this office:

_2008_

First elected to any office:

_2008_

First run for office:

_2006_

How did you raise money/name awareness/make political connections?

"I first ran for State Representative in 2006. I had never been involved in politics before so I didn't know anything about how to run. So I knocked on every door to gain name recognition, since I was running against a 16 year incumbent, who was also the chairman of one of the most powerful financial committees. I didn't get much party or financial (assistance) from any groups or organizations - just family and friends. I lost by a handful of votes.

"The people I talked with were impressed that I knocked on their door. In fact, I knocked on every door in the district 2-3 times - over 15,000 homes. Because most campaign signs are some version of red, white or blue. I decided to make mine yellow and purple. People started to identify me by those colors. I still continue with that theme today.

"I ran against the same opponent in 2008. However, this time I only knocked on doors of people registered to my same party and independents. I also received contributions from several outside sources. Plus we had a very good top of the ticket which I was able to ride some coat tails. This time we won by a handful of votes."

Ruth Briggs King

Office:

State Representative

Where:

Delaware (Dist. 37)

Elected to this office:

2009

First elected to any office:

2009

First run for office:

2009

What's the biggest piece of advice you'd give a political newbie?

"The number one rule, for me, was to be the candidate. This meant ensuring I had the right team and letting the team accomplish their goals individually and collectively. The best advice I can offer is to be sincere and honest. I truly enjoy the campaign process (which, I feel you are always in the campaign process). Everyone has a story and I believe you need to listen to the story and engage with the people. I have told some other candidates, 'put away your cell and blackberry. When you are with the people, be with the people.'"

Mathias Harter

Office:

Mayor

Where:

La Crosse, Wisconsin

Elected to this office:

2008

First elected to any office:

2008

First run for office:

2008

What advice did someone else give you that helped you through your first campaign?

"The best advice I was given in my first political campaign was, 'It's always best to be the underdog', and along with this, 'Always work like you're one vote behind.'"

Jim DeCesare

Office:

State Representative

Where:

Kentucky (Dist. 21)

Elected to this office:

2004

First elected to any office:

2004

First run for office:

2004

What advice did someone else give you that helped you through your first campaign?

"Look a person square in eye and ask for their vote. If you don't ask you will not get it."

Brent Yonts

Office:

State Representative

Where:

Kentucky (Dist. 15)

Elected to this office:

_1996_

First elected to any office:

_1984_

First run for office:

_1984_

**What's the biggest piece of advice you'd give a
political newbie?**

"My advice to a political newbie is to have an
established goal; be persistent by never giving up;
constantly be aware of what the people are talking about,
asking for and needing; communicate clearly, often and
every way possible – by letter, by weekly columns, by
responding to inquiries by telephone, fax, email and
otherwise at your elected office site; and being very
visible in the community, involved in everything.

"After being elected, get involved in everything
you can. As an elected official, you need to serve on as
many committees as you can, ask questions, raise issues
and promote policy changes to improve the performance

of government. Never be afraid to tackle an issue, but be

prepared for the unexpected when you do tackle it."

Robert Byrnes

Office:

Mayor

Where:

Marshall, Minnesota

Elected to this office:

1992

First elected to any office:

1986

First run for office:

1986

How did you raise money for your campaign?

"In my first run for mayor I had two opponents. I received contributions of $200 from a number of people who disliked the other candidates running for office. I used that money to put a couple ads in the paper. I was successful in that election. In the next five times I was re-elected, I did not raise any money, and my only expenditures were the $5.00 filing fee and putting a small thank you ad in the local paper after the election."

Mike Winder

Office:

Mayor

Where:

West Valley City, Utah

Elected to this office:

2009

First elected to any office:

2005

First run for office:

2005

What advice did someone else give you that helped you through your first campaign?

"A state legislator friend of mine encouraged me to think of your campaign as two parts(I envision it like the Asian yin and yang symbol of balance): get people who vote anyways, and get them to vote for you; and get people who are inclined to vote for you, and get them to vote. These are two very different and equally important exercises, especially in local races where the voter turnout will be much less than a presidential race. People who are inclined to vote for you include your neighbors (hopefully), people with demographic similarities, people with ideological similarities. Focus on educating these people when elections are, encouraging them to get out the vote. I did 24 different auto call messages once, each customized to different voting locations, so not only was I reminding them to vote, but I told them exactly where they go to vote.

"As for the other half of the yin and yang, getting people who vote anyway and get them to vote for you, think of it as a dart board. I used the voter history database and gave voters 1 point for voting in an even numbered year, 2 points when they vote in a municipal election year and 3 points when they vote in a municipal primary election. Then, in a simple Excel spreadsheet, I add up each voter's points and sort the list highest to lowest. What you then have is a list of the most likely to vote people--in order! The perfect voters are the people who always vote. They are the center of your dart board and deserve personalized attention and persuasion from the candidate. They are going to vote (they never miss), so make sure they will vote for you. The next group of likely voters are the next ring on your dart board. They deserve a personalized phone call. The next layer deserves mail pieces, but you probably won't have time to call them. The final layer deserves seeing your yard signs as they drive through the town, but don't waste your limited resources on sending mail pieces to people who never vote in local races. This prioritization will help you immensely. For example, I had $2000 to do a mailing once. It would allow me to reach 1200 homes. So I used my prioritization list and mailed to the 1200 most likely to vote homes.

"Another value of a most-likely-to-vote list is in personal contact. I realized that in municipal elections in my town the voter turnout was around 13% of registered voters. That means that if I went knocking doors about 1 in every 9 houses had someone inside likely to even vote in the city election. But I realized that with my most-likely-to-vote rankings I could sit down one night and call the fifteen most likely to vote people in the city. The next night I could personally call the next dozen most likely to vote people. If someone wasn't home, I could leave a personalized voicemail (i.e., 'Hello Smith family! I hope things are well on Mulberry Street today. This is Mike Winder, running for mayor of West Valley City. I would love to have your support on Nov 8 to help keep our city moving in the right direction. Please call me on my cell phone if you have any questions or suggestions on how to make our city better. My number is ------. Thanks, again, Smith family and have a great night!'

"The likely to vote people were randomly spread throughout the city geographically, so my touch points were sprinkled all over, instead of just the street I would have been knocking doors on. I experimented with this in my city council race, but did it full bore during my mayoral race. In fact, it proved so much more effective than knocking on doors; I never knocked a single door in my entire mayoral race! Moreover, as a young father of four children I found that I could eat dinner with my family, escape to my back porch for an hour or more of phone calls, come back inside to help put kids to bed, and then back outside to call for a bit. I didn't have that flexibility knocking doors. Also, I found that people were ok taking phone calls up until 9:30, but didn't want to answer a door much past 8:30, so my productive time each nugget grew by an hour."

Paul C. Lambi

Office:

Mayor

Where:

Westville, Missouri

Elected to this office:

2004

First elected to any office:

2001

First run for office:

2001

What did you learn as you were running your first campaign?

"I learned everything I know about public service and running for public office from the Autobiography of Benjamin Franklin. I have read it every year for 30 years.

"Get to know Ben! It is a very short book, if you read his original version. He distills 50 years of incredible accomplishments to a little over 100 pages. First lesson: humility."

Jim Farley

Office:

Mayor

Where:

Crystal River, Florida

Elected to this office:

2010

First elected to any office:

2004

First run for office:

2004

What's the biggest piece of advice you'd give a political newbie?

"I'm often approached by people who want to run for local office. The question I ask them is, 'where does your name recognition come from?' Usually they get a puzzled expression because they have none, or they didn't think that was important. Well, it's not only important, it's critical. Whatever level your campaign aspirations take you to, city, county, district, people have to recognize your name and attach a favorable connotation to it. In my run for mayor, one of the candidates opposing me was, by and large, unknown in the community. His campaign slogan was, 'New Face, New Vision.' He lost by a wide margin because no one knew the face or the name, and he didn't successfully articulate a 'new' vision. I was Police Chief in Crystal River for four years before running for City Council. As chief I was very active in the community and everyone got to know my name. I won the city council seat by a landslide without knocking on a single door. During six years as councilman I did the same, having a very public profile and continuing a positive reputation. I was rewarded by easily defeating two other candidates for Mayor. You don't have to have been police chief. If you're not known, spend two years building name recognition before you run for anything. Attend every public event you possibly can, particularly fund raisers. Volunteer in the community, there are so

many opportunities. Join a service club, such as Rotary, that offers fabulous networking opportunities with the movers and shakers in the community. Write letters to the editor. Attend city council and county commission meetings and regularly speak at the podium during the public input segments of the agendas. Make sure your point is clear and well founded because these meeting are generally covered by the press. Use every opportunity to be seen and heard in a positive way anywhere and everywhere in your community. It will be a tough couple of years, but the reward could be you hosting an election victory party!"

Scott Eckstein

Office:

Mayor

Where:

Bloomfield, New Mexico

Elected to this office:

2006

First elected to any office:

2004

First run for office:

2004

What did you learn as you were running your first campaign?

"The importance of a door-to-door campaign. It takes lot of time to go door-to-door, but it is extremely rewarding. A door-to-door campaign will give you a grass roots look into what the real issues are. You will not only learn a tremendous amount about your constituents concerns, but you will be further rewarded with likely voters. Voters are far more likely to vote for someone they have met, than someone they have not. They will also spread the word (word of mouth), which won't cost you a cent."

Dick Gleason

Office:

Mayor

Where:

Auburn, Maine

Elected to this office:

2009

First elected to any office:

2006

First run for office:

2006

How did you make political connections?

"I have never had any political aspirations. In both cases, when I ran successfully for city council and mayor, it was because I was asked.

"I think the reason I was asked is because I have shown a lifetime of interest and hard work in the communities in which I have lived.

"The eventual effect is that networking makes friends."

Bill Otto

Office:

State Representative

Where:

Kansas (Dist. 9)

Elected to this office:

_2004_

First elected to any office:

_1984_

First run for office:

_1984_

How did you win your election?

"I retired from teaching. I got $3,000 unused sick leave and printed my tri-fold paper. I made yard signs and road signs hand made from donated scrap wood and paint (that I made myself). I went door to door to almost every door. But I have also lived almost all my life in my district...

"When I ran in '04, I actually had better name recognition in many areas than the five term guy that was there. I never made it personal; I just put forth his voting record and said how I would do things different.

"Any ads I run have a clear position and a message, never just vote for Bill Otto...

"I use electronic media and never miss a parade, where I actually make a float, not just show up. I always pass out candy to the kids and talk to the people. I face people down and do not fear telling the truth."

<u>Bob Hartwell</u>

Office:

State Senator

Where:

Vermont (Bennington Dist.)

Elected to this office:

2006

First elected to any office:

2006

First run for office:

2004

How did you raise money/name awareness/make political connections?

"Fundraising bedevils most campaigns but is necessary to survive any seriously contested race; in my four campaigns for the Vermont legislature, I have held at least 10 fundraisers at homes of people I had known previously and I knew to be supportive.

"My approach has been not to put my own funds into my campaigns; so far I have been successful which I believe leaves voters with the fair impression that my financial support arguably mirrors general support. Generally I have taken contributions from persons and entities whose interests I have supported keeping in mind that any contribution in excess of $100 must be reported in detail to the Elections Division of the Vermont

Secretary of State and posted on the agency's web site for all to see.

Every contributor receives a personal thank you as soon as possible after my receipt of the contribution, and a complete record is maintained of all contributions so that I can ask again as another campaign begins. There are several dozen repeat contributors. When the time comes in the late winter and early spring of an election year, asks are personally tailored wherever possible to refer to those topics or issues of particular interest to a contributor to the extent these are known."

Mike Gabbard

Office:

State Representative

Where:

Hawaii (Dist. 9)

Elected to this office:

2004

First elected to any office:

1984

First run for office:

1984

What advice did someone else give you that helped you through your first campaign?

"I was advised by seasoned politicians to spend as much time as I could before the election going door-to-door. This is really a key to success. While I was running for City Council I knocked on every door in my district, over 30,000 doors, and I knocked on every door almost 3 times while running for State Senate. The opportunity to meet people face-to-face, at their homes and hear first-hand their ideas, their concerns, meet their kids and their dogs, etc. is invaluable. Some people will offer you cold drinks, a 5 course dinner, and talk your ear off for an hour, while others will slam the door in your face. But, most people really appreciate that you made the effort to come to their door, introduce yourself, personally hand them your brochure, and really listen to them. People remember that. I still get calls to this day where someone will say, 'I remember you, Mike. You came to my door', even though it was 9 years ago. It's really powerful. You also have to try to do what you can to remember people. Use whatever means you have to remember people's names. People will expect you to know them if they come up to you in the store, even if you only met them once briefly. "

Tamara Jenkins

Office:

Mayor

Where:

DuPont, Washington

Elected to this office:

_2007_

First elected to any office:

_2007_

First run for office:

_2007_

How did you raise money/name awareness/make political connections?

"Brand your message. Define vehicles for public outreach.

"Realize that together (with your team and supporters) you will make a difference.

"Have a well-organized campaigned and support group.

"Focus on the pure, powerful and positive. Shed the negative. Focus on where you are going. People want to be part of something awesome … a forward moving machine.

"Positive leaders attract more of the same.

"Define your core message. Keep in terms of odd numbers ... for example, 3 items, 5 items. People tend to remember in odd numbers.

"Keep the message simple.

"Network with groups, organizations and individuals that share the same values. For example, PTA, business associations, neighborhood coffee meetings, attend community events, volunteer at community events and so on.

"Go to the local hang outs reading the community issues and talking to people. The best form or advertisement is word of mouth."

Jerry Miller

Office:

Mayor

Where:

Winona, Minnesota

Elected to this office:

_1994_

First elected to any office:

_1980_

First run for office:

_1980_

What's the biggest piece of advice you'd give a political newbie?

"I would tell them, 'quit what you're doing, go out on a bus and go from stop to stop and meet people.'

"You have the internet, which is good, but you have to knock on every door. I would go down Main Street and introduce myself to everyone. Perception is everything."

Frank Lucente

Office:

Mayor

Where:

Waynesboro, Virginia

Elected to this office:

2010

First elected to any office:

2008

First run for office:

1980

What advice did someone else give you that helped you through your first campaign?

"I asked a former sheriff for some advice when I was first running for office. He told me that running for office was like being a tomato. He said, 'What's the first thing you think of when you think of a raw tomato?'

"'Green?' I said.

"'Yes, it's green,' he said. 'If you're determined, you'll get elected, but you'll be green like a tomato.'

"'Then once you're elected, you'll have a couple terms where everybody likes you. You'll be like a ripe tomato. '

"'Then what happens? It gets rotten. Like that rotten tomato, you'll create enemies and it's probably time to get out.'"

Harry Parrish

Office:

Mayor

Where:

Manassas, Virginia

Elected to this office:

_2008_

First elected to any office:

_1996_

First run for office:

_1996_

What's the biggest piece of advice you'd give a political newbie?

"If you're not already, talk with as many people as possible and let them know you're running. Talk with the chamber of commerce, talk to your local Kiwanis groups, talk to existing elected officials, talk to everybody.

"It's a simple thing, but sometimes simple things are hard to accomplish."

Peter Corroon

Office:

Mayor

Where:

Salt Lake County, Utah

Elected to this office:

_2004_

First elected to any office:

_2004_

First run for office:

_2004_

What's the biggest piece of advice you'd give a political newbie?

"The first thing someone will ask you is why you are running for office. The time to reflect on this is before the question is asked. Be ready for it. If you stumble on this question, the citizen will not consider you any further.

"You have to be able to ask people for money. If you are not willing to do so, don't bother running for office unless it is a small race and you don't need much money.

"You have to be willing to spend the time away from your hobbies, work and family in order to campaign and once you get elected, it gets worse. If you have important family commitments or are too invested in work or weekend hobbies, it will be difficult to run a

campaign and serve in office.

"Be yourself. People appreciate genuine people."

Charles Langlinais

Office:

Mayor

Where:

Broussard, Louisiana

Elected to this office:

1990

First elected to any office:

1988

First run for office:

1986

What's the biggest piece of advice you'd give a political newbie?

"If you have no money and no connections, get in with an established politician. Ride his tails and go door to door, that is how I did it"

Joe Markley

Office:

State Senator

Where:

Connecticut (Dist. 16)

Elected to this office:

_2010_

First elected to any office:

_1984_

First run for office:

_1984_

What's the biggest piece of advice you'd give a political newbie?

"If you're new to politics, don't try to impress people by telling them how much you know--show them instead how much you want to learn. Ask questions and listen to the answers; try not to speak unless you have something to say. Always ask who else you should sit down with--keep building your circle of contacts outward, turning contacts into friends and friends into allies. Mark no one down in your mind as an enemy: alliances shift from issue to issue, and the more people you can work with, the better you can serve the cause."

Carolyn Eslick

Office:

Mayor

Where:

Sultan, Washington

Elected to this office:

2002

First elected to any office:

2002

First run for office:

2002

What advice did someone else give you that helped you through your first campaign?

"Keep your closet clean at all times. Integrity and honesty are the only ways to live your life, private and political. Work six days a week on the political trail and take one day off with the family."

Dave Kiffer

Office:

Mayor

Where:

Ketchikan, Alaska

Elected to this office:

2008

First elected to any office:

2008

First run for Office:

2009

What's the biggest piece of advice you'd give a political newbie?

"People often underestimate the value of humor in political discussion. They see it as a sign of weakness or even worse, a lack of seriousness of purpose. It is just the opposite. When debate gets intense we can lose sight of the fact that person on the other side is really just another person like our self. He or she just has a different point of view. Often a well-placed witticism can be a reminder to tone down the anger a bit and a shared laugh can be a reminder that we are more alike than not and can build on that.

"It works wonders with non-politicians as well. Recently, I saw a constituent angrily approach a fellow local legislator. 'I wouldn't vote for you if you were St.

Peter himself,' the constituent muttered. There was a pause and the politician replied, gently and with a smile, 'If I were St. Peter, you wouldn't be in my district.' There was a pause, then a laugh, the real discussion began."

Barbara Bollier

Office:

State Representative

Where:

Kansas (25ᵗʰ District)

Elected to this office:

2010

First elected to any office:

2010

First run for office:

2010

What did you learn as you were running your first campaign?

"The biggest thing I learned during my campaign was going door-to-door. People are tired of bitter politics. They want someone who can communicate, someone who can work with the other side.

"I focused on that once I heard it. But you have to be honest. I was that person, I was always honest – if you're not, you can't remember what you told the last person. Then you're in trouble."

Shari Buck

Office:

Mayor

Where:

North Las Vegas, Nevada

Elected to this office:

2009

First elected to any office:

1999

First run for office:

1999

What's the biggest piece of advice you'd give a political newbie?

"I would tell anyone wanting to run for office, that it is well worth it. It will take time and commitment. I believe the more people the candidate can speak with face to face, the better.

"That means walking neighborhoods, knocking on doors, attending community meetings, etc. That is how I won my first campaign against an incumbent. She had more money than I, but we outworked her.

"Most people will become paralyzed with fear, intimidated, insecure. You have to push through all those emotions and keep going. I walked 6 days a week for 6 months in order to win my first seat. It was a good weight loss program also, because I lost 20 lbs."

Part 3
Securing a political appointment

Philip Murphy

Office:

State Senator

Where:

North Dakota (Dist. 20)

Appointed to this office:

2011

First elected to any office:

N/A

First run for office:

1984

How did you go about receiving your political appointment?

"In early December of 2011, our longstanding state senator decided that his wife was too debilitated for him to leave and serve the upcoming session in our capital. It is a little over 200 miles from our small town to Bismarck. We in North Dakota have only one session every other year which can last up to 80 working days. Starting in the first week of January, this takes us through April. As the general election had been held and the session was about three weeks away, our Democratic District 20 Executive Committee accepted eight applications for the position in the approximately ten days they had before winnowing through the essays to arrive at a final three. I made the cut with a newly retired female speech pathologist with no prior political experience, a veteran legislator who had been redistricted out ten years earlier after serving at least three terms – I had run in 1984 for the state house and did not win at that time.

"While I had stayed involved, mostly at the periphery, my wife (that I had met campaigning in 1984) and I raised three children. Two were in college and one was a senior in high school. I am a high school economics, history, psychology, government and geography teacher. I garden, read, hunt, fish, golf and have walked or biked to work every day for over 15 years. ANYWAY, the three of us spoke in turn to the Executive Committee in mid-December. The Committee included the chair, current legislators and officers. The experienced legislator was on the committee as was his wife and his neighbor. He had three of the ten votes locked up and I thought it was a mere formality to vote before his coronation. Here is how I remember: On the first ballot, the chair announced that the candidate with the most votes could sit out the second round. Then the low person would get voted out. The female and I got three each, he got four. On the second ballot we tied 5-5. On the third I won 6-4 and she was gone. On the fourth ballot, the veteran and I tied 5-5 and the committee was perplexed. The chair directed that they continue to vote. On the fifth ballot, I won 6 to 4. I may never have been so surprised, humbled and excited in one moment in my life."

Jim Reynolds

Office:

Mayor

Where:

Eagle, Idaho

Appointed to this office:

2010

First elected to any office:

N/A

First run for office:

N/A

How did you go about receiving your political appointment?

"First, I am a retired businessman with no political history whatsoever. I was appointed, not elected, when the previous mayor resigned prior to his term in office. After months of wrangling between the Council Members, no one could muster the necessary votes to assume to position, and they opened it up to the community. Of 15 entries, it came down to two of us and they selected me…

"The only possible advice I could offer is: be yourself, be honest and completely transparent."